LIFE IN A
VIKING TOWN

JANE SHUTER

Heinemann Library
Chicago, Illinois

Customer Service 888-454-2279
Visit our website at www.heinemann classroom.com

Originated by Modern Age
Printed in China by WKT Company Limited

09 08 07 06 05
10 9 8 7 6 5 4 3 2 1

Library of Congress Cataloging-in-Publication Data

Shuter, Jane.
   Life in a Viking town / Jane Shuter.-- 1st ed.
      p. cm. -- (Picture the past)
   Includes bibliographical references and index.
   ISBN 1-4034-6440-5 (hc) -- ISBN 1-4034-6447-2 (pb)
   1. Vikings--Juvenile literature. 2. City and town life--Juvenile literature. I. Title. II. Series.
   DL65.S53 2004
   948'.022--dc22
                                              2004025846

Acknowledgments:
The publishers would like to thank the following for permission to reproduce photographs: AAAC p. **16**; AKG pp. **14**, **20** (Schijtze/Rodemann); Bergin Field and James p. **8**; Bridgeman p. **28**; British Museum p. **24**; Corbis pp. **6** (Richard T. Nowitz), **12** (Archivo Iconografico); National Museum of Denmark p. **11**; Werner Forman pp. **10**, **22**, **29** (National Museum of Iceland, Reykjavik); York Archaeological Trust pp. **13**, **18**, **23**.

Cover photograph of a wood carving showing a Viking blacksmith at work, reproduced with permission of Picture Desk.

Every effort has been made to contact copyright holders of any material reproduced in this book. Any omissions will be rectified in subsequent printings if notice is given to the publishers.

The paper used to print this book comes from sustainable resources.

Any words appearing in bold, **like this**, are explained in the Glossary.

Contents

Who Were the Vikings?

The Vikings lived in Norway, Sweden, and Denmark, more than 1,000 years ago. They had a reputation for being **raiders** who attacked without warning. There were many different groups of Vikings, each with their own leader. At first, the Vikings lived in small **settlements**. Then they began to live, work, and **trade** in towns. The Vikings who lived in towns had different lives than those who lived in the countryside.

Look for these: The chessmen show you the subject of each chapter. The picture of a runestone shows you boxes with interesting facts, figures, and quotes about life in a Viking town.

TIMELINE OF EVENTS IN THIS BOOK

A.D. 700 Vikings spread across Norway, Denmark, and Sweden

A.D. 780 First Viking raids on England

A.D. 795 First Viking raids on Ireland

A.D. 799 First Viking raids on France

VIKINGS MOVE ACROSS EUROPE, SAILING UP MAJOR RIVERS A.D. 800–850

A.D. 800 Birka (Sweden), Hedeby (Denmark), Kaupang (Norway) start to grow as trading towns

A.D. 836 Vikings set up Dublin, which becomes a trading town in the 880s

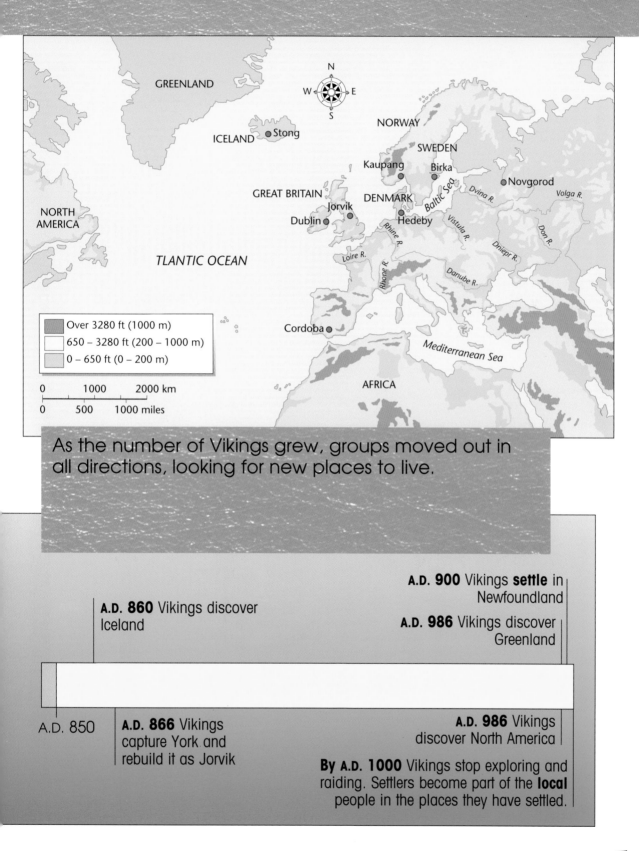

As the number of Vikings grew, groups moved out in all directions, looking for new places to live.

A.D. 860 Vikings discover Iceland

A.D. 900 Vikings **settle** in Newfoundland

A.D. 986 Vikings discover Greenland

A.D. 850

A.D. 866 Vikings capture York and rebuild it as Jorvik

A.D. 986 Vikings discover North America

By A.D. 1000 Vikings stop exploring and raiding. Settlers become part of the **local** people in the places they have settled.

Viking Towns

The earliest Vikings lived in small farming **settlements**. However, as they began to **trade**, some settlements grew into trading places. More and more people came to these trading places, so they grew into towns. Often, these towns had walls and gates to keep out **raiders** from other Viking groups.

Once Vikings began to live in towns, there were more strangers around. They began to lock away their valuables with keys like the ones shown here.

The Vikings did not call builders when they wanted a new home. They and their neighbors built the house together. Most of the homes were very similar. Homes in towns often doubled as **workshops**.

Viking craft workers had workshops in their homes. In this picture, you can see a blacksmith and a woodworker in the yards of their homes.

Who Lived Where?

The street names in **Jorvik** tell us that different craft workers lived in different parts of town. Viking craft workers **specialized** in making just one thing. They made shoes, cups, or knives and sold them to other people out of their **workshops**. All the shoemakers lived in one area, all the cup makers in another area, and so on.

NAMES

Some Viking words look like modern words, but they don't always mean the same thing. The Viking for "cup makers" was *kopari* and "street" was *gata*. So *Coppergate* was the cup makers' street, not where the copper makers worked.

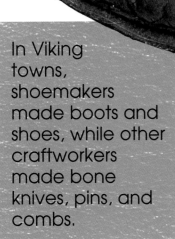

In Viking towns, shoemakers made boots and shoes, while other craftworkers made bone knives, pins, and combs.

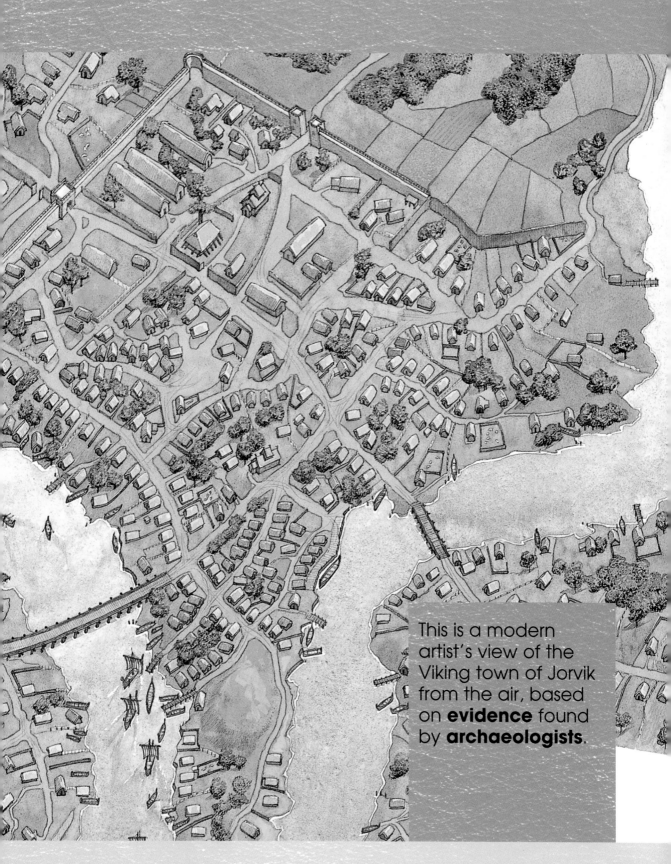

This is a modern artist's view of the Viking town of Jorvik from the air, based on **evidence** found by **archaeologists**.

Trade was important to the Vikings, and it helped their towns to develop quickly. The Vikings traded some things **locally**, in their own towns. These were everyday things such as shoes, pottery, wooden chests, tools, and weapons. Craft workers sold them to people in the town or to people from nearby **settlements**.

SLAVES

When they attacked other places, the Vikings often captured women and children, and sometimes men too. They then kept these people as **slaves**, or sold them when they next went trading.

The Vikings sometimes used silver to pay for things. The value was based on the weight of the silver. Viking traders took their own scales and weights, like these, to check other traders' weighing.

The Vikings also traded with people from far away. They traded **goods** they had plenty of, such as furs, honey, and fish, for goods such as silk and spices. They traded at least as far west as Greenland, as far east as Russia, and as far south as the North African coast. The goods they bought sometimes came from even farther away. Goods from as far away as India have been found in Viking graves.

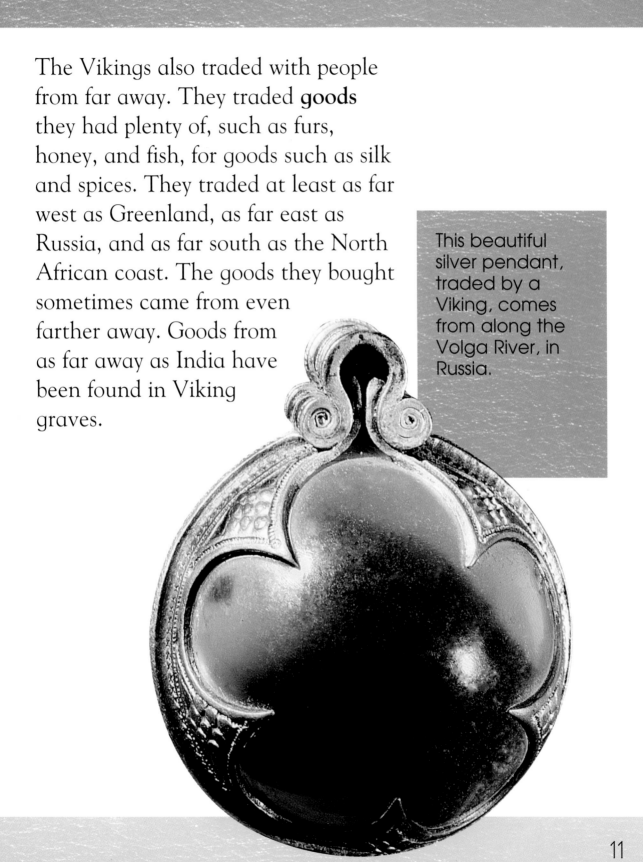

This beautiful silver pendant, traded by a Viking, comes from along the Volga River, in Russia.

Work

Most people in towns were **specialized** craft workers, making things such as pots. People came from all around to buy their **goods**. These craft workers had **workshops** in the front of their home, on the street. They sold from their workshops or a stall. People who had no skills tried to make a living by fetching and carrying for the workshop owners, or working as servants in the homes of the rich.

The craft worker who made this **brooch** probably charged a lot for it. He had to pay a lot for the gold he used to make it. He also had to spend a lot of time learning how to work with gold.

The Viking towns of Hedeby, in Denmark, and **Jorvik**, have both been **excavated**. **Archaeologists** found **evidence** of craft workers making objects from metal and bone in both these towns. They also found evidence that jewelers, glassmakers, potters, woodworkers, and ropemakers had worked there. There were also many leatherworkers, who made boots, shoes, purses, and belts.

LEARNING A CRAFT

Viking craft workers learned their **trade** by working for a skilled craft worker from about the age of ten. Workshops often had three or four workers at different stages of learning their craft.

Bone objects, like these, were quickly made from cheap materials, but they had to be sold cheaply, too.

13

Warriors

Viking men did not just have one job. They all had to be **warriors** and **raiders** too. The king of each Viking group had to be able to lead all the men in battle. Viking men went exploring and raiding throughout the summer, leaving the women to run things at home. They always took their weapons, expecting to have to fight somewhere along the way.

Well-made Viking swords were often handed down from father to son. Some were even given names like "*foe biter*", which means "destroy the enemy."

The people of the town took turns guarding the town walls and searching the **local** countryside if they thought they might be attacked.

WEAPONS

The Vikings fought with swords, spears, and axes. They had metal helmets and wooden shields edged with metal or leather to protect them. Shields had to reach from shoulder to knee and were usually round.

Homes

Houses in Viking towns were built on pieces of land with fences around them. What they were made from, and how they were made, depended on where the town was. In cold places, the Vikings dug out the floor to below ground level, which made homes warmer. In Greenland, homes were made from stone covered with dirt and grass. In Great Britain and Europe, homes were made from wood and thatch, or straw.

OUTSIDE THE HOUSE

Viking homes in towns usually had pens for chickens and animals as well as a toilet outside the house. They often had a garden for growing fruit and vegetables, too.

Buckets were important in a Viking home. All the water for washing and cooking had to be fetched from a nearby well.

Viking women made cloth for the family clothes on looms.

The cooking **hearth** had stones around the edge for safety. It was the only heating.

Wide benches down either side, made of wood or dirt, were used for sleeping or sitting.

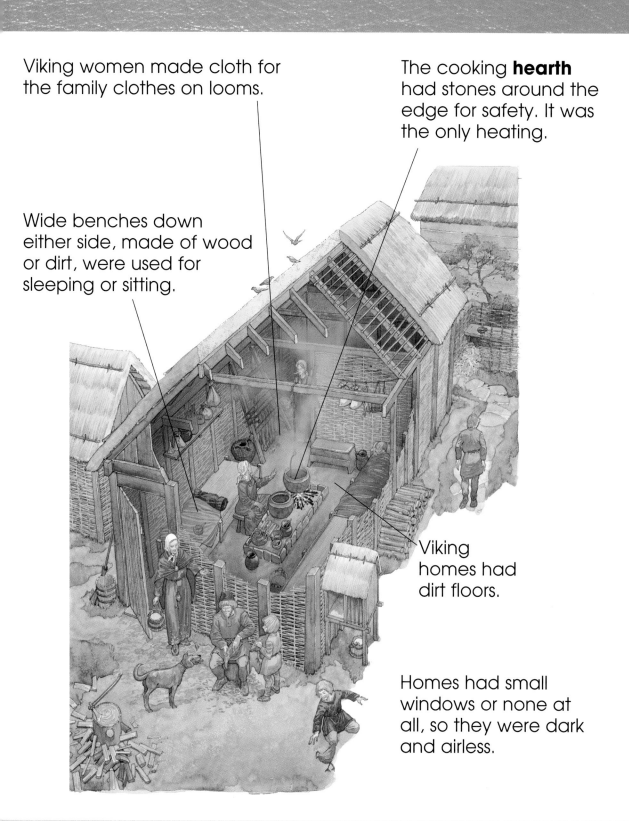

Viking homes had dirt floors.

Homes had small windows or none at all, so they were dark and airless.

Family Life

Families were very important to the Vikings. In early Viking times, most people in a **settlement** were related. They lived in large family groups and took pride in knowing their family's history. The men of different families arranged marriages between their children, but a Viking girl was allowed to reject a possible husband. Divorce was allowed if a couple was unhappily married.

WOMEN

Viking women did not go to war with men. They were not **raiders**. They did not trade, either. But they could own their own property and run the family farms and businesses while their husbands were away.

Women rubbed stones, like these, against cloth to help smooth it.

Children in towns did not begin to learn a **trade** until about the age of ten. Children born in a farming settlement would start helping with work on the farm from a very young age.

Boys who lived in towns often helped their fathers when they were very small, before going away to learn a trade.

Education

Children were brought up in the family home until they were about ten. After that, boys were often sent to live with relatives or friends of the family. There they would learn a **trade** and how to fight. The sons of important Vikings did not need to learn a trade, but they may have learned to read or studied the law.

A LEADER'S SKILLS

One leader lists the things he had learned: "I can write well, I can read, and mend a sword easily. I can ski, fire arrows, and row well. I can recite poetry and play music." A **saga** said a leader also had to be a brave **warrior**.

Writing was important to the Vikings. They used knives to carve letters called runes onto stone or wood.

Viking girls learned to run a home, while boys learned a skill. Childhood did not last long. A boy was treated as an adult from about the age of twelve and some girls were married at that age.

This boy is learning to be a blacksmith. Before learning to shape metal, he learned to get the fire to just the right heat. This was done by blowing air into it with a leather bag called a bellows.

Free Time

In most parts of the Viking world, the long dark winters shortened the working day. So, the Vikings had a lot of free time. The Vikings played different board games. They loved poetry and storytelling. Often, the women wove cloth and the men carved wood while listening to a story. They liked clever tricks with words too, like riddles and proverbs.

RIDDLES

A good riddle was a rhyming description of an ordinary object. They could be very long and difficult. This is a shorter riddle:
On the way a miracle: water becomes bone.

(Answer on page 30.)

This is a game where one side has a king and his **warriors**. The other side has no king but more warriors. They have to try to capture the king.

In the time of the Vikings, stories were not written down. So people had to learn them by heart. At feasts, storytellers called skalds told stories called **sagas**. Most skalds were men. The stories they told could go on for hours. The stories usually rhymed, to make them easier to remember. Skalds also had to be able to make up stories about the latest events in their group, such a victory in battle.

The Vikings made their own music. Their instruments were made of wood and bone. Many people made their own.

Clothes

Most Vikings wore the same kinds of clothes, usually made from wool. The women of the family spun, dyed, and wove the cloth themselves. They used vegetable dyes. The colors could be quite bright to begin with, but soon faded. Rich Vikings could buy expensive fabrics, like silk, from **traders** in towns.

SILK

Only kings and rich people could afford clothes made from silk. They bought the silk at the market and **slaves** made the clothes for them. Because the silk came all the way from China, it was very expensive.

The Vikings had simple hairstyles. They carried combs with them, to keep their hair and men's beards tidy.

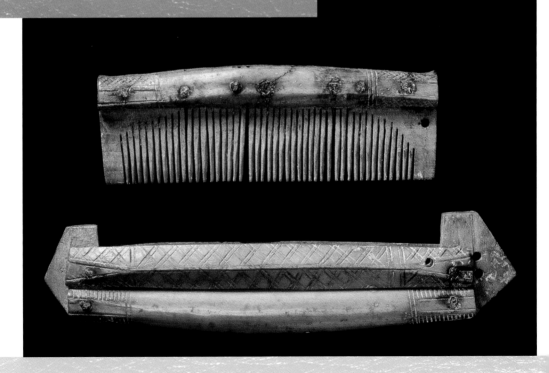

Women and girls wore long dresses covered with an apron when they were working. Men and boys wore pants and a **tunic**. Cloaks tied with a **brooch** were the usual sort of covering for going outdoors. Shoes, boots, and belts were made from leather.

Vikings dressed to fit the weather. In cold places they lined their boots with fur. They also changed the way they dressed to fit in with **local** people. Traders did this, and so did **settlers** who moved to newly discovered lands.

Food and Drink

The Vikings ate two meals a day, in the morning and in the evening. They cooked over an open fire on a **hearth** in the middle of their houses, using iron pots and pans. They ate a lot of meat, fish, bread, cheese, and vegetables. They grew and raised most of the food themselves.

FEASTS

Vikings held feasts to celebrate marriages, victories in battle, and other important events. Feasts could go on for days. Different food was cooked—whole animals were roasted and special sauces were made.

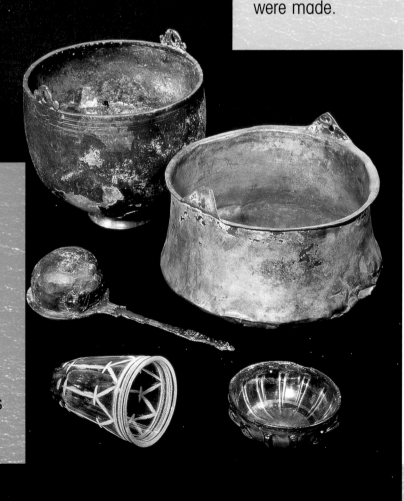

Some iron pots stood on legs over the fire. Others were hung from the roof on a chain that hooked onto the handle of the pot. You can see the holes for handles on these pots.

Berry Pudding

The Vikings would have cooked this dish over an open fire, but you can do it in an oven instead.

WARNING: Do not cook anything unless there is an adult to help you.

1 Pre-heat the oven to 225°C (425°F).

2 Mix the salt and the two flours together.

3 Slowly add the milk, stirring, then whisking, with a fork as you go.

4 Melt the butter in a shallow baking tray in the oven.

5 Stir the berries into the batter and pour the batter into the pan.

6 Cook for about 20 minutes. Take it out when it is golden brown.

Religion

The early Vikings believed in many different gods and goddesses. They thought that these gods and goddesses controlled everyday life. They had to be kept happy with prayers and presents. The Vikings imagined the gods as living together in heaven in a big family group, arguing, fighting, and making up, just like human families do.

THE MAIN GODS

Thor	god of storms
Odin	god of war
Frey and Freya	god and goddess of growing things

This hammer-shaped charm is the symbol of the god Thor, the god of thunder (because thunder makes a hammering sound). It has a Christian cross on it too, because some Vikings were Christians.

Some Vikings became Christians. Sometimes this was because some Christians would only **trade** with other Christians. Sometimes a Christian king who defeated a Viking in battle would make him change religions. Many Christian Vikings still worshiped their old gods, too, even though Christianity said not to do this.

Vikings who became Christian built churches like this one to worship in. The Vikings probably went to special places outdoors to worship their other gods.

Glossary

archaeologist person who looks for objects from long ago to study how people lived in the past

brooch piece of jewelry to pin onto clothing

evidence something that tells you what happened

excavate when things are dug out of the ground, layer by layer. This is usually done by an archaeologist, who takes notes about what she or he finds

goods things that are bought, made, and sold

hearth fireproof, safe place indoors to build a fire for cooking or heating

Jorvik Viking city in the north of England, now the city of York

kingdom all the land and people that are controlled by one leader

local of a certain area

raiders people who go to a place to take things by force from the people who live there

saga Viking adventure story

settle move from one place to live in another

settlement place where people live and bring up their families for many years

slave person who is bought and sold by someone, to work for that person

specialized to do just one job, not many jobs

trade person's job; or the selling or swapping of goods

tunic clothing shaped like a T-shirt that came to about the knees

warrior person trained to fight in battle

workshop place where several people work together to make something

Answer to the riddle on page 22:

an icicle

Further Reading

Books

Chapman, Gillian. *The Vikings*. Chicago: Heinemann Library, 2000.

Rees, Rosemary. *The Vikings*. Chicago: Heinemann Library, 2002.

Shuter, Jane. *The Vikings*. Chicago: Heinemann Library, 2003.

Index